Google Power Search

Stephan Spencer

D1451420

O'REILLY®

Beijing · Cambridge · Farnham · Köln · Sebastopol · Tokyo

Google Power Search

by Stephan Spencer

Copyright © 2011 Stephan Spencer. All rights reserved.
Printed in the United States of America.

Published by O'Reilly Media, Inc., 1005 Gravenstein Highway North, Sebastopol, CA 95472.

O'Reilly books may be purchased for educational, business, or sales promotional use. Online editions are also available for most titles (*http://my.safaribooksonline.com*). For more information, contact our corporate/institutional sales department: (800) 998-9938 or *corporate@oreilly.com*.

Editors: Mary Treseler and Jem Matzan	**Cover Designer:** Karen Montgomery
Production Editor: Jasmine Perez	**Interior Designer:** David Futato
Technical Editor: Hamlet Batista	**Illustrator:** Robert Romano
Proofreader: O'Reilly Production Services	

July 2011:   First Edition.

Revision History for the First Edition:
2011-07-15	First release
2011-10-21	Second release
2011-11-18	Third release

See *http://oreilly.com/catalog/errata.csp?isbn=9781449311568* for release details.

ISBN: 978-1-449-31156-8

[LSI]

1321629115

Table of Contents

Google Power Search

Introduction

You probably use Google every day to find things—news, technical support, events, tips, research documents, and more. What would happen if you were to master Google's powerful search refinement operators and lesser-known features? Over a year's time you could save days scouring over irrelevant results. Or if results are more important than time, then perhaps the allure of finding well-hidden market research and competitive intelligence on the Web through cleverly-designed queries is more enticing. In either case, this book will show you how to find what you need quickly and accurately.

With over a trillion URLs in its index, Google is a treasure trove of information. Yet finding just the right document out of this massive pool of URLs—the one that answers your question—can be difficult without using Google's search-refinement operators. Operators are explained in detail in this book, starting with Chapter 1.

Advanced search operators are covered in Chapter 2. This gives you a proper introduction to *filetype:, intitle:, inurl: site:*, and *daterange:*. In Chapter 3, you'll learn to put your new search refinement tools into practice with a real-world example. You'll also learn about various features in Google's graphical interface, such as Search Within Results, Similar Pages, SafeSearch filtering, spelling corrections, "I'm Feeling Lucky," and the Advanced Search page.

Chapter 4 covers Google's many other search properties, including iGoogle, Google Reader, Google News, Google Maps, Google Product Search, Google Groups, and Google Images, as well as some useful third-party sites powered by Google.

In Chapter 5, some Google gurus explain a few theoretical advanced search workflows that you may find helpful when developing your search strategies.

Chapter 6 moves beyond end-user search, and explains the tools, operators, and tips that are particularly useful to search engine optimization (SEO) professionals in their quest for higher Google rankings for their Web sites.

Conventions Used in This Book

The following typographical conventions are used in this book:

Italic
> Indicates new terms, URLs, email addresses, filenames, and file extensions.

`Constant width`
> Used for program listings, as well as within paragraphs to refer to program elements such as variable or function names, databases, data types, environment variables, statements, and keywords.

`Constant width bold`
> Shows commands or other text that should be typed literally by the user.

`Constant width italic`
> Shows text that should be replaced with user-supplied values or by values determined by context.

 This icon signifies a tip, suggestion, or general note.

 This icon indicates a warning or caution.

Using Code Examples

This book is here to help you get your job done. In general, you may use the code in this book in your programs and documentation. You do not need to contact us for permission unless you're reproducing a significant portion of the code. For example, writing a program that uses several chunks of code from this book does not require permission. Selling or distributing a CD-ROM of examples from O'Reilly books does require permission. Answering a question by citing this book and quoting example code does not require permission. Incorporating a significant amount of example code from this book into your product's documentation does require permission.

We appreciate, but do not require, attribution. An attribution usually includes the title, author, publisher, and ISBN. For example: "*Google Power Search* by Stephan Spencer. Copyright 2011 Stephan Spencer, 978-1-449-31156-8."

If you feel your use of code examples falls outside fair use or the permission given above, feel free to contact us at *permissions@oreilly.com*.

Safari® Books Online

Safari Books Online is an on-demand digital library that lets you easily search over 7,500 technology and creative reference books and videos to find the answers you need quickly.

With a subscription, you can read any page and watch any video from our library online. Read books on your cell phone and mobile devices. Access new titles before they are available for print, and get exclusive access to manuscripts in development and post feedback for the authors. Copy and paste code samples, organize your favorites, download chapters, bookmark key sections, create notes, print out pages, and benefit from tons of other time-saving features.

O'Reilly Media has uploaded this book to the Safari Books Online service. To have full digital access to this book and others on similar topics from O'Reilly and other publishers, sign up for free at *http://my.safaribooksonline.com*.

How to Contact Us

Please address comments and questions concerning this book to the publisher:

O'Reilly Media, Inc.
1005 Gravenstein Highway North
Sebastopol, CA 95472
800-998-9938 (in the United States or Canada)
707-829-0515 (international or local)
707-829-0104 (fax)

We have a web page for this book, where we list errata, examples, and any additional information. You can access this page at:

http://www.oreilly.com/catalog/9781449311568

To comment or ask technical questions about this book, send email to:

bookquestions@oreilly.com

For more information about our books, courses, conferences, and news, see our website at *http://www.oreilly.com*.

Find us on Facebook: *http://facebook.com/oreilly*

Follow us on Twitter: *http://twitter.com/oreillymedia*

Watch us on YouTube: *http://www.youtube.com/oreillymedia*

Credits

Hamlet Batista and Jem Matzan both provided guidance during the creation of this ebook.

Hamlet is Altruik's Chief Search Strategist. He is also a respected commentator on search trends and has written extensively at hamletbatista.com (*http://hamletbatista .com*). As an inventor, he was granted US Patent #7805428 for an SEO automation product.

Jem is a professional writer and editor in Orlando, Florida. You can reach him at *jem@jemmatzan.com*.

Content Updates

November 18, 2011

- Added Google+ Realtime Search feature to Chapter 4.
- Added Google Image Search upload feature.
- Removed the + operator from Chapters 1 and 5.
- Removed colloquialisms and other familiar speech from the narrative in the Preface and Chapters 1 and 2. More narrative edits will follow in subsequent book updates.
- Added additional interview material from a Google Search Education Fellow, Tasha Bergson-Michelson.

CHAPTER 1

Refining Your Searches

If your search yields millions of search results, then your search query is too broad. Rather than skim over many pages of search results, use these search refinement tips to provide more focused results:

- **Multiple words:** Avoid making one-word queries.
- **Case insensitivity:** There's no need to capitalize.
- **Superfluous words:** Drop overly common words.
- **Exact phrases:** Put quotes around phrases.
- **Word order:** Arrange your words in the order you think they would appear in the documents you're looking for.
- **Singular versus plural:** Use plural if you think the word will appear in that form in the documents you're looking for.
- **Wildcard:** * can substitute for a whole word in a multiword search.
- **Number range:** .. between numbers will match on numbers within that range.
- **Punctuation:** A hyphenated search word will also yield pages with the un-hyphenated version. Not so with apostrophes.
- **Accents:** Don't incorporate accents into search words if you don't think they'll appear in the documents you're looking for.
- **Boolean logic:** Use *OR* and - to fine-tune your search.
- **Stemming:** Google may also match on variations of your search word; to turn this off, use double quotation marks to define an exact word or phrase.
- **Synonyms:** ~ in front of a word will also match on other words that Google considers to be synonymous or related.

Multiple Words

The first key to refining a search is to use a multiple-word query. A one-word search query isn't going to give you a targeted a search result. As a simple example, searching for *ohio car buyer statistics* instead of *statistics* will obviously yield a smaller and more specific set of search results. Start with the shortest relevant search query, see what results you get, then refine it by adding more words and operators after that if the results are too broad.

Case Insensitivity

Searches are case insensitive for the most part, so capitalizing the word Ohio in the above example is unnecessary, as it would return the same results. Note that search operators such as *site:* must not be capitalized (operators are explained in more detail later in the book) but *OR* should be capitalized if you mean to use it as a Boolean operator rather than a keyword.

Superfluous Words

Overly common words like *the, an, of, in, where, who,* and *is* are known as *stop words.* Google usually omits these words from a query unless it detects some kind of special case scenario, such as if they are part of a common phrase, a name of a place, the title of a book, etc.

Avoid formulating your query as a question. A search like *how many female consumers in ohio buy cars?* is not an effective query. Questions invariably contain superfluous words that probably won't appear in the text of the documents you are searching for (such as the word *many*). Thus, a large number of useful documents will have been eliminated.

Exact Phrases

If you're looking for a phrase rather than a collection of words interspersed in the document, put quotes around your search query. Enclosing a query in quotes ensures that Google will match those words only if they occur within an exact phrase. Otherwise, Google will return pages where the words appear in any order, anywhere on the page. For example, a *market research* query returns many more (but less useful) results than *"market research"* would.

You can include multiple phrases in the same query, such as *"market research"* consultants *"new zealand"*; such a query would match on documents that contain the word *consultants* in front of or behind the phrase *market research*, but giving preference to pages where *consultants* appears after *market research*.

Don't make a query out of a whole phrase if you aren't sure about the word order. In the example of *"market research" consultants "new zealand"* you might be tempted to simply put one set of quotes around the whole set of words (like so: *"market research consultants new zealand"*). This would return a nearly empty result set because it's not a likely order of words used in natural language.

Word Order

It's important to consider the order of the words you use in your search query, because it can affect not only the number of results, but the relative rankings of those results as well. Pages where those words/phrases appear in the order given in your search query will appear higher in the results.

Singular Versus Plural

Consider whether the pages you seek are more likely to contain the singular form or the plural form of a given keyword, and then use that form in your search query. For example, a search for *car buyers females statistics* does not return nearly as good a set of results as *car buyers female statistics*.

Wildcard

The asterisk acts as a wildcard character and allows you to omit one or more words in a search phrase. This is useful in multiple ways. You can substitute a word or name that you can't remember or which has multiple spellings. You can also use the asterisk in market research where you want to concentrate on specific keywords that are frequently used as part of phrases, such as *ohio * cars*, in which the asterisk would represent many useful words like used, new, wrecked, classic, or specific properties (red, convertible, etc.) or brands (Honda, Ford, etc.). If you wish to learn more about marketing your own books, you'd be better off with a search for *marketing * books* than *marketing books*, as the latter would return more results discussing books about marketing.

Asterisks can be used as a substitute only for an entire word—not for a part of a word.

The asterisk is even more helpful when used within an exact phrase search. For example, *"standards * marketing"* would match pages that match for the phrases *standards for marketing, standards in marketing*, as well as *standards and marketing*, to name a few.

When you put numbers between the *, Google will display the product of those two numbers. This is an exception to the wildcard use case.

Number Range

Your Google search can span a numerical range; you indicate the range by using two dots between two numbers, which could be years, dollar amounts, or any other numerical value.

For example, a search for *confidential business plan 2008..2011* will find documents that mention *2008* or *2009* or *2010* or *2011*. The query *confidential business plan $2000000..$5000000* will match documents that mention dollar figures anywhere in the range of $2 million to $5 million, even if commas are present in the numbers.

As a shortcut, you can leave off the high end and Google will assume infinity. For example, *100..* will match on any number greater than or equal to 100. Use *0..100* to match numbers less than or equal to 100.

Note that currency symbols such as *$* change the nature of a number. A search for *Nikon 400* will yield different results than *Nikon $400*.

Punctuation

Other than these special characters (wildcard and range indicators), most punctuation gets ignored. An important exception is the hyphen. A search query of *on-site consulting* will be interpreted as *onsite consulting OR on-site consulting OR on site consulting*. The hyphen indicates a strong relationship between two words; the underscore symbol also connects two words under most conditions.

Another important exception is the apostrophe, which is matched exactly if contained within the word. So, *marketer's toolkit* will return different results from *marketers' toolkit*, but the latter will be equivalent to *marketers toolkit* (i.e., without the apostrophe).

Accents

Accents are yet another exception. A search for *internet cafés manhattan* will yield a markedly different set of results than *internet cafes manhattan*. For search terms and phrases that include accents, always perform your search with and without the accent to ensure a complete set of results.

Boolean Logic

You may find that you want to match on both the singular and plural forms of a word. In that case, you can use the *OR* search operator, as in *"direct marketing consultant OR consultants"*. Note that the *OR* should be capitalized to distinguish it from *or* as a keyword.

You may be wondering if, since there is an *OR* operator, there is an *AND* operator as well. Indeed there is. However, it is not necessary to specify it, because it is automatically implied. So don't bother with it.

Google also offers an exclusion operator, but it's not called *NOT*. It's the minus sign (-). It works as you might expect, eliminating from the search results the subsequent word or quote-encapsulated exact phrase. For example, *confidential "business plan" OR "marketing plan" -template* will not return pages in the results if they mention the word *template*, thus effectively eliminating the sample templates from the results and displaying a much higher percentage of actual business plans and marketing plans. (As an example of a query with a phrase negated instead of a single word, consider *"marketing plan" -"business plan".*)

The *OR* operator can be abbreviated as a pipe symbol (|). Thus, the previous search query can be fed to Google as *confidential ("business plan" | "marketing plan") -template.*

Google has exceptions for all of these operators. For instance, if the word "or" is part of a phrase, Google will probably detect it as such and not treat the "or" as an operator. Similarly, the + symbol can be part of a common word or term (such as the C++ programming language or the Notepad++ text editor), or as an addition operator when it appears between two numbers; Google will display their sum. When the − is used between two words as a hyphen, Google will not treat it as a "not" operator; it will treat the two words as one hyphenated term.

Stemming

Sometimes, Google automatically matches on variations of a word. This is called *stemming*. Google does this by matching words that are based on the same stem as the keyword entered as a search term.

So, for the query *electronics distributing market research*, Google will match pages that don't mention the word *distributing* but instead a variation on the stem *distribute*: e.g., the keywords *distributor*, *distributors*, and *distribution*.

You can disable the automatic stemming of a word by putting quotes around it. For instance, *electronics "distributing" market research* will not match on *distribution*, *distributors*, *distributor*, and so on.

Synonyms

You can expand your search beyond stemming to incorporate various synonyms too, using the tilde (~) operator. For instance, *market research data ~grocery* will also include pages in the results that mention *foods*, *shopping* or *supermarkets*, rather than *grocery*.

CHAPTER 2

Google Search Operators

Google is capable of much more than simple search; it can make your work life more productive and easier on a number of levels.

Chapter 1 has already explained several ways to refine your Google searches through simple operators and other tricks that involve a search query. This chapter explains how to use advanced search operators, which enable you to refine a search by limiting the index by Web location, content type, and various search metadata (title, link text, post date, etc.).

All operators are case-sensitive, so be sure to use all lowercase letters (the iPhone's Web browser will try to capitalize the first letter of every sentence, so make sure you go back and correct it before executing your query).

Here's a quick list of the most useful Google search operators, followed by a more in-depth explanation of each:

Table 2-1. Google search operators

Operator Description	Format Example	Description
filetype:	marketing plan filetype:doc	Restrict search results by file type extension
site:	google site:sec.gov	Search within a site or domain
inurl:	inurl:marketing	Search for a word or phrase within the URL
allinurl:	allinurl: marketing plan	Search for multiple words within the URL
intext:	intext:marketing	Search for a word in the main body text
allintext:	allintext: marketing plan	Search for multiple words within the body text of indexed pages
intitle:	intitle:"marketing plan"	Search for a word or phrase within the page title
allintitle:	allintitle: marketing plan	Search for multiple words within the page title
inanchor:	inanchor:"marketing plan"	Search for a word or phrase within anchor text
allinanchor:	allinanchor: marketing plan	Search for multiple words within anchor text

Operator Description	Format Example	Description
daterange:	marketing plan daterange: 2454832-2455196	Restrict search results to pages indexed during the specified range (requires Julian dates)
related:	related:http://www.abc.com/abc.html	Display pages of similar content
info:	info:http://www.abc.com/abc.html	Display info about a page
link:	link:http://www.abc.com/abc.html	Display pages that link to the specified page
cache:	cache:http://www.abc.com/abc.html	Display Google's cached version of a page
define:	define:viral marketing	Define a word or phrase
stocks:	stocks:aapl	Display stock quote and financial info for a specified ticker symbol
{area code}	212	Display location and map of an area code
{street address}	123 main, chicago, il chicago, il chicago, etc.	Display a street map for a specified location
{mathematical expression}	35 * 40 * 52 520 miles in kilometers, etc.	Do a calculation or measurement conversion
{package tracking ID}, {flight number}, etc.	valid tracking ID	Track packages, flights, etc. using valid tracking IDs
{time in location}	time in london, england	Shows the local time in the specified location
{weather in location}	weather in titusville, florida	Shows a multiday basic weather forecast for the specified location
{movies in location}	movies Philadelphia, pa	Returns movie showtimes that are playing at all theaters in this location
{flights to/from location}	flights Tucson	Returns flight times to, from, or between the locations specified
{sunset/sunrise in location}	sunset in Key West, FL	Returns the expected time of sunset or sunrise in the given location, in that place's local time
{sports team}	San Francisco 49ers	Shows the score from the game this sports team is playing in, or the schedule for future games if this team isn't playing today
earthquake	earthquake	Shows the latest earthquake information around the world

filetype:

You can restrict your search to Word documents, Excel documents, PDF files, or PowerPoint files by adding *filetype:doc, filetype:xls, filetype:pdf,* or *filetype:ppt,* respectively, to your search query.

Want a great PowerPoint presentation on email marketing that you can repurpose for a meeting? Simply query Google for *email marketing filetype:ppt.* Need a marketing plan template? Since the template would most likely be a Word document, cut through the web page clutter with a search of *marketing plan template filetype:doc.* (Don't link to your own marketing plans if you don't want them showing up in Google's index.)

In fact, Google allows any extension to be entered in conjunction with the *filetype:* operator, including htm, txt, php, asp, jsp, swf, etc. Google then matches on your desired extension after the filename in the URL. Note that there is no space after the colon when using this operator. You can use *ext:* instead of *filetype:* —they do the same thing.

site:

You can search within a site or a domain by adding the site: operator followed by a site's domain name to your query. For example, you could search for *email marketing* but restrict your search to only pages within the MarketingProfs site with a query of: *email marketing site:www.marketingprofs.com.*

You can also add a subdirectory to the end of the domain in a site: query. For example *email marketing site:http://www.marketingprofs.com/tls*

To conduct a comprehensive search of all of the associated subdomains of a domain, omit the www and instead specify only the main domain. For example, a search for *site:yahoo.com* would encompass not just www.yahoo.com, but also movies.yahoo.com, travel.yahoo.com, personals.yahoo.com, etc. The site: search operator works even when just the domain extension (like .com, .org, .gov, or .co.uk) is specified. Thus, you can restrict your search to .com sites with *site:com,* to .gov sites with *site:gov,* or to .co.uk with *site:co.uk.*

Combining Boolean logic with the site: operator will allow you to search within multiple sites simultaneously. For instance, *email marketing (site:marketingprofs.com | site:marketingsherpa.com | site:marketingpower.com)* searches the three sites simultaneously. The site: operator can be specified by itself without other search words to get a list of all pages indexed, such as site:www.marketingprofs.com. Again, note that there is no space after the colon when using this operator.

Use this approach to simultaneously search competitor sites for keywords of particular relevance (e.g., related products you want to monitor). Then either create a bookmark to easily monitor the index or create a Google Alert (to be explored later in this book) to receive an email any time the index changes.

The *site:* operator works outside of ordinary Web search—it also works with Google Images, Google Product Search, and Google News.

inurl:

Use the *inurl:* operator to restrict the search results to pages that contain a particular word in the Web address.

This can be especially useful if you want Google to display all the pages it has found within a particular directory on a particular site, such as *inurl:ftp site:http://www.kellogg.northwestern.edu* or all the pages with a particular script name, such as *inurl:ToolPage site:http://www.vfinance.com*. Again, there is no space after the colon when using this operator.

allinurl:

This operator is similar in function to the *inurl:* operator, but is used for finding multiple words in the Web address. It eliminates the need to keep repeating *inurl:* in front of every word you want to search for in the URL.

For instance, *allinurl: china exporting* is an equivalent and more concise form of the query *inurl:china inurl:exporting* to find pages that contain the words *china* and *exporting* anywhere in the URL, including the filename, directory names, extension, or domain. There IS a space after the colon when using the *allinurl:* operator.

intext:

Searches for a word in the main body text. This is used in a similar fashion to *inurl:*. For instance, if you wanted to find only pages that referenced Stephen Hawking and relativity, you might search for *stephen hawking intext:relativity*.

allintext:

Searches for multiple words within the body text of indexed pages. This is used in a similar fashion to *allinurl:*.

intitle:

Use the *intitle*: operator (such as *intitle:marketing*) to look for documents where your specified word or phrase matches in the page title. This is the hyperlinked text (usually blue) in the Google search result, which also appears in your browser's topmost bar.

If you want to find Microsoft Word documents in which the document title (located within Properties under the File menu in Word) includes the phrase *marketing plan*, you would use the query *intitle:"marketing plan" filetype:doc*. Follow the *intitle*: operator with a word or a phrase in quotes, without a space after the colon.

allintitle:

This works like *intitle*: but searches for multiple words in the title. For instance, use *allintitle: channel conflict online retail* to search for documents that contain all four of those words in the title. Note that there is a space after the colon when using this operator.

inanchor:

The *inanchor*: operator will restrict your search to pages where the underlined text of inbound links matches your search word. For example, if you wanted to search for merchandising but confine your search primarily to home pages, *merchandising inanchor:home* would do the trick, since most sites link to their own home pages using the link text of "Home."

Follow the *inanchor*: operator with a word or a phrase in quotes, without a space after the colon.

allinanchor:

This works like *inanchor*: but searches for multiple words in the link text. For example, the query *web metrics allinanchor: download trial* would invoke a search for pages relating to web metrics that have the words *download* and *trial* in the link text.

Note that there is a space after the colon when using this operator.

daterange:

The *daterange*: operator restricts the search results to pages added or updated within the specified date range. Unfortunately, it only accepts Julian dates, which makes it less user-friendly than it could be. You can find Gregorian-to-Julian date converters online, e.g. here: *http://www.fourmilab.ch/documents/calendar*

You'll usually find it easier just to do your search first without a date range, then use the custom date range options in the "More search tools" area of the result page.

related:

related: queries show pages that are similar to the specified Web page. Follow this operator with a Web address, such as *related:http://www.marketingprofs.com*, and you would find pages that are related to the MarketingProfs home page. This is identical to the Similar link in the bottom left of the Preview pane of each search result.

info:

An *info:* query lets you know whether the specified page is known by Google, and it provides the title and a snippet (if available), a link to the page, a link to a cached version of the page (see below for an explanation of this), and a link to view pages that link to the specified page.

Supply a Web address after this operator, such as *info:http://www.marketingprofs.com*.

link:

The *link:* operator returns a sampling of pages (i.e., a small subset of the total) that link to the specified Web page. Follow this operator with a Web address, such as *link:http://www.marketingprofs.com* to find pages that link to the MarketingProfs home page.

Use the *link:* operator in Google Blog Search and you can obtain a fairly comprehensive list of blog posts that link to the specified web page.

cache:

The *cache:* operator provides a snapshot view of a web page as it looked when Googlebot last visited the page. Follow this operator with a Web address, such as *cache:http://www.marketingprofs.com* to view the page that Google has cached. Note that Googlebot must have downloaded the page in order for this to work.

There is more information on Google's cache later in the book.

define:

This is a useful operator for quickly obtaining several definitions from various online glossaries. Curious about the definition of "tipping point"? Simply type *define: tipping point* into Google.

stocks:

Wondering how your competitor is performing on Wall Street? Enter this operator followed by a ticker symbol to retrieve financial information, including latest stock quotes from Google Finance. Note that in most circumstances this operator is optional. Google figures out if the query is a ticker symbol pretty well. An exception to this is *dell* versus *stocks:dell*.

{area code}

Google also offers an area code look-up. For example, enter *313* and Google returns the geographic location and map corresponding to that area code.

{street address}

Queries in the format of a street address automatically return street maps. Enter a full street address, or a ZIP code, or a city and state. For example, *123 east main street, madison, wi* or *53703* or *madison, wi* are all valid map-based Google searches.

{mathematical expression}

Enter any valid mathematical expression, and Google's calculator function will interpret it for you. It will even do currency and measurement conversions for you, such as *100 dollars in euros*, or *8 ounces in cups*. Learn more about what other syntax is valid at the Google calculator page at *http://www.google.com/help/calculator.html*

{package tracking ID}, {flight number}, etc.

Enter a valid package tracking ID into Google and you can also track packages. Or, supply an airline and flight number to Google, and it will return flight times. Google will even return information about a car's history if you query it with the VIN (vehicle information number).

In fact, Google will spit back all sorts of interesting information when it recognizes a particular number format, such as a patent number, FAA airplane registration number, UPC Codes, or FCC Equipment ID.

{time in location}

Google will display the local time and date for any location on Earth—all you have to do is tell it where. This takes into account time zone and daylight savings calculations according to the location's rules. You can pass a city and country name, or a postal code.

{weather in location}

Much like the time feature, Google can display a weather forecast for a given location, specified by a city and country, or a postal code. The top result is a four-day basic weather forecast.

{movies in location}

Google has information on show times from most local theaters in any given location. When you click on the first result in a movies search, the modified result page will sort shows by movie, genre, day, time, and theater.

{flights to/from location}

If you search for *flights Philadelphia*, you will get a table of outbound flights to Philadelphia's largest airport (PHL) from a wide array of origins. You can switch this around and find out what flights are outbound from PHL by searching for *flights from Philadelphia* instead. Lastly, you can specify both an origin and a destination, and if nonstop flights exist between those two points, Google will print the airlines, flight numbers, and departure and arrival times.

CHAPTER 3

Initial Market Research Using Google

Now that you are familiar with the range of Google operators to refine your searches, it's time to put the knowledge into practice in the real world. It's also a good time to delve a little deeper into the essential features of the Google interface.

In this chapter, we'll apply some interesting Google tactics to search for information about the food industry. Then I'll explain the essential features of the Google user interface—the virtual place where you spend most of your time interacting with Google—and apply those to our search example as well.

A Search for Market Research in the Food Industry

Let's imagine that your task is to find market research on the food industry. Specifically, you are looking for details on frozen vegetable consumption within the United States —including consumer demographics, the size of the market in dollars, and so on. You are writing a business plan for the potential launch of a line of frozen organic peas.

Your strategy is to drill down into the results with a refined search query.

You might try a search on *market research* to start your quest, just to see what Google suggests and recommends as query refinements. However, that's typically going to be far too generic a query for a direct search. *Market research food industry* is better, but still there's a lot of noise in the search results to sift through.

A search for *market research frozen vegetables* would be better still, but not as laser-focused as it could be. Let's try it regardless, just for fun.

That search yields, first off, a page from marketresearch.com (*http://marketresearch .com*) listing research reports, and the last one listed is called "Food Markets in Review: Frozen Vegetables," published this year. Sounds promising!

But after clicking through, we find that the report costs $195. I forgot to mention that your budget is $5. Thus, buying this report is out of the question.

So let's do a quick check to see if a PDF of the report is floating around somewhere on the Net free for us to download. No such luck: a search for the title *"food markets in review: frozen vegetables" filetype:pdf* only yields an excerpt of the report: the three-page Table of Contents.

Let's further narrow our search by wrapping the phrases in quotes—*"market research"* and *"frozen vegetables"*—and by restricting matches to PDF documents, since those are likely to offer meaty reports with lots of factual information.

So our new search becomes *"market research" "frozen vegetables" filetype:pdf*, and we hit pay dirt: search result no. 5 is a 15-page report called "The Demand for Organic Agriculture: A Study of the Frozen Pea Market."

Once we examine the document, however, we find it a bit dated. It refers primarily to data from the 1990s. So we can further refine the search to include mentions of 2009 or 2010 or 2011, which could be done as follows: *"market research" "frozen vegetables" filetype:pdf 2009..2011.*

Unfortunately, many of the top search results returned are from other countries, such as France and China, whereas we're only concerned with the United States. Because the United States can be referred to in so many ways, we could append to our query these different forms as a group of *OR* statements at the end. Thus, the query would look like *"market research" "frozen vegetables" filetype:pdf 2009..2011 u.s. | u.s.a. | usa | united states | america.*

However, I have a better idea. Rather than listing geographical names, we could include the names of two prominent competitors in the U.S. market.

Thus, our search becomes *"market research" "frozen vegetables" filetype:pdf 2009..2011 "birds eye" "green giant"*—and we get a solitary result back. And, thankfully, it's a good one. It includes a chart and graph with a few years of annual sales figures by frozen vegetable/fruit manufacturers, along with some future projections.

More Searching

Let's continue looking for stats, but take a different tack entirely. We'll use the tilde operator to capture synonyms as well, because the documents we're looking for could be referring to frozen food, or frozen foods, or frozen meals, or frozen vegetables, or frozen peas, and so on.

Thus, a query of *"frozen ~vegetables | ~food" "annual sales" 2009..2011* should do the trick. And it does! It yields a fantastic document in the top search result. That document delivers a range of statistics from the American Frozen Food Institute, including frozen vegetable sales broken down by type of vegetable; it also offers some interesting consumer information, such as this nugget: on an average trip to the supermarket, 94% of shoppers purchase frozen food sometimes, with 30% always buying frozen food.

Phew. Job well done, and it didn't require sifting through hundreds of irrelevant search results.

We got some good results in this hypothetical exercise. Yet, right at our fingertips, there would have been more that we could have extracted had we utilized some of the functions built into the Google user interface. Maximizing what you get out of the Google search results requires that you master this range of functionality.

Let's take a closer look, then we'll wrap up by applying what we've learned about these functions to our hypothetical quest.

Alternative Date Range and Sorting Method

An alternative to the .. operator is available through Google's advanced search options, which include searching and sorting by date. Just click the "More search tools" to the left of the search results for a list of advanced options, then click any of the predefined time ranges, or define your own. Once you've done that, you can sort the result set by relevance to the search term, or by date from newest to oldest. The time spans that Google provides are for the past day, two days, week, month, and year.

The most recent results will show up if you select the Latest option. The SERP associated with Latest will be updated in real time as new results show up for that search query.

Finding Documents People Thought Weren't Public

If you're feeling particularly nosy, if you've got industrial espionage in mind, or if you just want to get some ideas on how to craft documents that are not typically available, you can make creative use of the *filetype:* operator. Try these if you're looking for confidential business plans:

> *confidential business plan filetype:pdf*
> *confidential business plan -template filetype:doc*

Forrester Research typically sells its research reports. Once someone has gotten their hands on one of Forrester's PDFs, though, it might find its way to the Web by accident. Two somewhat uncommon words that have tended to appear in Forrester reports are *grapevine* and *endnotes*. Try searching for those words, plus whatever your search term is, and use the *filetype:* operator to narrow down the results to just PDFs; you just might be able to get a relevant Forrester report for free.

Just enter this following query to obtain Forrester reports on a range of topics:

> *forrester research grapevine endnotes filetype:pdf*

Key Features of the Google User Interface

It's surprising how many useful features are tucked into such a simplistically elegant interface as Google's. Making the most out of Google is as much about knowing the nuances of this interface as it is about mastering Google's query operators.

Figure 3-1 shows what's in the standard web search page if you have not customized it or logged into a Google account (the numbers correspond with the list below the graphic, and are explained in greater detail later in this chapter).

Figure 3-1. The default Google search page

1. **I'm Feeling Lucky:** Takes you directly to the first search result
2. **Images:** Takes you to Google Images, where you can search for photos and illustrations
3. **Videos:** Takes you to Google Videos, where you can view and search for video clips
4. **Maps:** Takes you to Google Maps, where you can search geographically, confining the results to a specified location, and get search results back that are pinpointed on a street map or satellite map
5. **News:** Takes you to Google News, featuring news articles in a variety of categories. Will take you directly to relevant search results for recent news items if you enter a query first
6. **Shopping:** Takes you to the Google Product Search page, where you can search online retailers and catalogs

7. **Gmail:** Free web-based email with gigabytes of free email storage
8. **More:** Offers access to Google's many other sites and features, such as Google Books, Google Blog Search, the Google Chrome browser, and much more
9. **Search Settings:** Change the number of search results displayed per page, use Google's language tools, access advanced search options, and other search settings
10. **Sign in:** Lets you create or log in to a Google account for more personalization of Google features and services
11. **Change background image:** Allows you to choose a background image for your Google home page
12. **Voice search:** If you are using the Google Chrome or Chromium browser and have a microphone connected and properly configured, you can use this feature to speak your search query in simple terms

Figure 3-2 shows the Google search results page, affectionately referred to as the "SERP" (an acronym for "search engine result page") by those in the search industry. Once again, the numbers correspond to the interface features in the list.

Figure 3-2. The Google search result page

13. **Spelling corrections:** Google automatically suggests more popular/likely spellings
14. **Cached:** A previously archived version of the web page listed in the Google search results

15. **More Results:** Additional matches from the same site
16. **Quick View and View as HTML:** Allows quick and easy viewing of non-HTML documents, viewable within your web browser
17. **+1:** Vote for this result if you feel it's particularly relevant to your search
18. **Ads:** Advertisers bid to be positioned here, and pay per click
19. **Tools and filters:** This section provides a wide variety of ways to expand or refine your search, as well as some useful sorting options. The available options will change quite a bit depending on what type of query you ran
20. **Instant previews:** The magnifying glass icon next to HTML search results will toggle thumbnail views for each result

Depending on what you searched for, sometimes you may also see results from Google News, Google Maps, Google Product Search, Google Blog Search, or Google Books embedded within the Google search results page.

Now let's take a more in-depth look at the default Google search and search results pages.

I'm Feeling Lucky

This is the button on the Google home page to bypass the Google search results page and jump straight to the first search result. This is particularly useful if you are confident that the first search result will be the right one.

For example, a search for *toyota* will undoubtedly yield Toyota's home page as the first result; so, if that's where you want to go, you might as well use the *I'm Feeling Lucky* button.

While the *I'm Feeling Lucky* button is still present on the static Google homepage, Google Instant puts it in the drop-down list from the search field. To access it, just use your mouse or arrow keys to highlight an item in the Google Instant list of suggested terms, and you'll notice I'm Feeling Lucky on the right side of the highlighted field.

Images

This link will take you to the Google Images search engine, which searches millions of images on the Web, including photos, illustrations, buttons, and clipart. If you click the Images link from the Google homepage, you'll go to the image search homepage instead. If you are on a search result page when you click Images, your search query will be re-executed for an image search.

Videos

This specialized search engine puts countless video files at your fingertips, including TV shows, movies, music videos, documentaries, video blogs, training videos, and much more. Some videos require payment to watch. Note that Google has discontinued the ability to upload your own videos here, but you can still share your own videos with their popular YouTube service (discussed in "YouTube" on page 34).

Maps

This is a great tool if you need to find local businesses or services in the United States, Canada, and many cities abroad, or if you want to geographically explore a region. It's especially handy when you're looking for restaurants within walking distance. Search using location names such as *toronto*, addresses such as *931 e. main st, madison, wi*, type of business such as *pizza*, or a combination of the above such as *hotels near lax*. And you can get driving directions, *lax to 92780* for instance. You can even conduct keyword searches that are restricted to the map region displayed on your screen. Google returns phonebook listings with associated web pages on the left and, on the right, the top results are all pinpointed on the map.

The map interface allows you to toggle between street maps, satellite images, and hybrid views of both. In addition, many areas are also available in a panoramic Street View mode with photos taken from a specially equipped vehicle. You can also smoothly pan around and zoom without the slow reloading of pages that you get with other mapping services like MapQuest.

News

This link will take you to the Google News service, which shows a range of top headlines and stories in a variety of categories. From there, you can also query the Google News archives, which will search countless news sources worldwide, including newswires, magazines, newspapers, and academic journals. The Google News index is updated continuously, but only includes stories from the past 30 days. For older stories, search the Google News Archive directly at *http://news.google.com/archivesearch*.

If you are already on a web search result page, click the News link at the top of the page to jump directly to Google News search results. Sometimes Google News results are embedded automatically in the main Google search results, depending on the search query used.

Looking for news related to a certain topic or event? Use the *related:* operator to see what Google thinks are relevant stories.

Shopping

This link will take you to Google Product Search, formerly known as Froogle, which includes products for sale across online catalog sites across the Web. Sometimes, Google Product Search results are embedded automatically in the main Google search results, depending on the search query used.

Gmail

Gmail is Google's web-based email service, which offers users gigabytes of storage absolutely free. POP and IMAP protocols are both supported too. It also has an additional social networking service called Google Buzz, with many features similar to Facebook and Twitter. Google Buzz allows you to broadcast messages and share links and content with selected groups of followers, follow other users, update your location and more.

More

This dropdown list will take you to Google's many other sites and services, such as YouTube, Google Labs, and Google Finance. We will explore many of these services later in this book.

Search Settings (Preferences)

This is the place to change the number of results displayed on search results pages, as well as other settings like your preferred language for search results. Or, if you just want to change the number displayed for a particular search, you can manually add *&num=* followed by any number from 1 to 100 (no spaces) at the end of the URL of any Google search results page (you must have Google Instant turned off for this to work). This will limit the results displayed per page to your specified number—for example, 25 search results for the query *marketing* will be displayed with the following URL:

http://www.google.com/search?q=marketing&num=25

From this screen, you can also turn off Google Instant and personalized search, and erase your web history.

Sign In (Google Accounts)

If you create and sign in to a personalized Google Account, you can take advantage of a wide range of personalization and customization options with many of Google's services. You'll need a Google Account to use services like Gmail and iGoogle. You don't have to be signed in for Google to personalize your search based on searches performed with this browser within the past 180 days, but if you do sign in, your entire search history affects the results, and it won't be tainted by searches done by others who have used this browser recently.

Voice Search

If you've got a microphone connected, turned on, and ready to pick up your voice, you can speak your search terms into the main Google search screen. Unfortunately, heavily accented non-American English will fool the speech-to-text algorithm. Even if you speak clearly, sometimes the right words aren't detected, or the wrong homonyms are used. And if you try to say anything you couldn't say in a G-rated movie, Google will replace all but the first letter of the term with asterisks to censor it out.

Change Background Image

If you're logged into your Google account, you can choose a background image for your Google home page. Google provides a number of images you can use, or you can upload pictures of your own.

Spelling Corrections

Google automatically senses misspellings and offers corrections at the top of the search results. Sometimes the search results will automatically include results for what Google thinks you're trying to spell. Simply click on Google's suggested correction to re-execute your search using the correctly spelled word.

Cached

Did you get all excited about a Google result just to find it leads to a File Not Found error, or is the site you're tying to access temporarily down? Fret no longer. Simply click on the Cached link next to the search result you want, and Google will retrieve the version of the document it downloaded and stored the last time its spider visited the page.

The cached feature is also handy because it will highlight on the page the keywords that you were looking for. Google even specifies in the top right corner of the page when it retrieved that page. Note that sometimes, at the top of the cached page, Google will display "these words only appear in links to this page." This happens because Google associates the underlined text of hyperlinks with the page that is being linked to.

If you need a cached page to load more quickly, or on a mobile device with limited screen space, append the *&strip=1* parameter to your Google cache URL, which will strip the images from the page, or simply click on the link on the cached page that says "Text-only version."

More Results

The Show More Results link sometimes appears under a search result when there are many additional documents from the same site that match your query. Clicking on this link will expand to show some more links from that same site. From there, clicking the *Show All Results* link at the bottom of the expanded section will conduct another Google search for your query, but the results will be exclusively from the one site.

This is equivalent to adding a *site*: operator to your query. Note that with More Results and the *site*: operator, the typical limit of two pages per site in a page of search results does not apply.

Quick View and View as HTML

When a search result is a PDF file, Word document, PowerPoint file, or Excel document, you can click on View as HTML to preview it as text extracted from the document.

+1

This button enables you to vote for relevant results. Google gives some level of consideration to these votes when weighting its search rankings and customizing your results.

Ads

Google advertisers bid against each other to be positioned here and are charged every time someone clicks on a link. The click-through rate in part determines which ads display at the top, in addition to the advertiser's maximum bid amount. The intention here is that the most relevant ads, according to Google's users, rise to the top over time.

Tools and Filters

The left side of the basic SERP provides a wide variety of ways to expand or refine your search, as well as some useful sorting options. The top section will show filtering options for different types of content, so you can see results just from Google News, Google Maps, or some of their other most popular types of searches. You'll also find a search tools section with a variety of options for limiting your search by other criteria like date ranges, or showing local results only. Some other interesting features worth mentioning here are:

Related searches
Shows you popular search terms that other Google users are looking for.

More Search Tools
Provides a range of search refinement options, such as: Sites with images, Related searches, Timeline, Visited pages, Not yet visited, Dictionary, Reading level, Social, Nearby, Translated foreign pages.

The options you see here will change according to the Google search tool you are using. For example, if you search videos, the options will allow you to filter your results by video quality and duration (among other options), while Google News results will include a wide range of selected date ranges and others. Furthermore, even within a standard search from the Google home page, you might see different filtering options and tools for different types of information in your query. For example, searches for *barack obama*, *green bay packers*, *how to remove grass stains*, and *best online prices for women's shoes* might all show slightly different options and filters.

Instant Previews

Clicking once on the magnifying glass will invoke Instant Previews, which will allow you to hover over any result to see a thumbnail view of its corresponding web page. This will give you a quick idea of what the page looks like without having to visit it. Instant previews can be handy in a number of unusual situations, such as when you remember visiting a site from a previous search but didn't bookmark it; you remember what it looked like but can't remember the URL. It's also helpful when you have to conserve bandwidth or are on a slow connection and don't want to take the time to visit each page and wait for it to load.

Other Google Interface Features

The following options are not shown for all search result pages, or are features that you can turn on manually.

Advanced Search

The Advanced Search page (available under the Search Settings icon on the top right) is a useful crutch if you want to refine your search but don't remember the search operators explained earlier in this guide. Searching within the title, URL, anchor links to the page, etc. are all supported. However, if you can recall the search operators discussed earlier, it's more efficient to use them from the main Google search box than to turn to Google's Advanced Search screen. Some of the more interesting options on this page make it easy for you to exclude words from your query, search for specific file types, and even search by usage rights (e.g., filter results to Creative Commons–licensed content).

Language Tools

The Language Tools page (available under the Search Settings icon on the top right) is where you can change your preferred language for the Google interface, translate phrases and pages, and choose the local Google domain for your country. You can also specify a language or languages to which to have search results translated.

The Snippet

The snippet is not really a "feature," per se—it's a traditional part of any search result page. The snippet is a block of text that represents your page content in the SERP. It is dynamically generated by Google at the time of the query, and will change depending on the nature of the search, though it is rarely longer than 156 characters. Snippet content is taken from page content (in various places), meta description tags, and sometimes the Open Directory.

Translate This Page

The Translate This Page link only appears in the search results next to documents that are in a foreign language. Bear in mind that machine translation will give a very inexact English version of the document; it's not always intelligible, but you can usually get the gist of what's being said on the page. The Google Translate engine also gives you options for translating into other languages.

Preview

The magnifying glass icon to the right of each search result will enable you to see a thumbnail preview of a page without having to visit the link.

Similar Pages

Follow the link in the bottom left of the Preview pane (accessible via the aforementioned magnifying glass icon) to display documents that Google considers similar to the document in the search result by executing a related search on its URL using the *related*: query operator.

Suggestions

Google's search box very effectively second-guesses what you are searching for before you finish typing in your search phrase and fills in the rest of the search term for you. In other words, just start typing and, with each keystroke, Google starts suggesting search keywords.

For example, if you type "buy c", Google lists search terms in what appears to be in order of search popularity, such as *buy cds, buy car, buy cars, buy cd, buy computer*, etc.

iGoogle

Customize Google's home page with your city's weather, your favorite team's scores, latest messages from your Gmail inbox, past search history, saved bookmarks, late-breaking headlines across numerous news sources and RSS feeds, and more.

Experimental Features

Google is constantly developing new features and services, and it almost never waits for any of them to be "done" before making them available to users. Sometimes Google engineers will push a new feature out into an existing search service without much (if any) warning, test it for a while to see if and how people are using it, then either change or remove it later. Features can appear or disappear in an instant, but actual Google services that the company wants to shut down are phased out for a long period of time before they go totally dark.

Google often makes new services available on an invitation-only basis. If you aren't extremely well-connected, you might not get an invite to a new service until it goes mainstream.

If a new feature isn't introduced and activated by default in its services, Google will put it into an experimental area so that users can find it on their own and choose to try it out. Each service has its own "experimental" or "labs" area. For the standard Google web search, that area is here:

> *http://www.google.com/experimental*

At any given time, you may find some interesting and useful features there.

Teasing Out More, Better Data

Let's now apply some of what we've learned about the Google interface to uncover even more material for our hypothetical research mission.

If you recall, we had found an excerpt of "Food Markets in Review: Frozen Vegetables." Now, by clicking on the Similar link within that search result's preview, we obtain a helpful list of relevant trade associations and press, such as the Food Marketing Institute, Grocery Manufacturers of America, American Frozen Food Institute, National Food Processors Association, and Prepared Foods magazine. That list could prove useful, so we'll make a note of those, but for the moment we'll put the list aside and continue our quest.

Remember that we didn't find the greatest of results with our *market research frozen vegetables* query. But perhaps we were too hasty in abandoning that search. Search results no. 4 and 5 didn't look like what we were after ("Frozen Vegetables in China" and "Research and Markets—Frozen Food"), but the site where they came from, researchandmarkets.com, looked promising.

So, using Google's More Results function, we further probed that site and found a report titled "US Frozen Vegetable—Research and Markets" as the sixth result, which covers market size, market segmentation, market shares, distribution, socioeconomic data, and forecasts. Unfortunately, the price tag is $240, a little steep for our $5 budget.

We haven't looked through news stories yet, so let's give that a go. When we specify a query of *competitor "birds eye"* and click the News link, we find some articles about Birds Eye, but also a lot of noise—news stories containing the idiomatic expression "bird's eye view." So we'll employ the minus sign (-) operator to eliminate those results, with a query of *"birds eye" -view*. Google returns an article from the Rochester Business Journal titled "Birds Eye, HMO Promote Healthy Eating," an article relevant to our research.

Let's use another method to locate additional relevant news stories. The query *"birds eye" -view site:news.yahoo.com* might yield some interesting results from Yahoo! News. Not much there, so let's expand our search and try *vegetable consumption site:news.yahoo.com* instead. The first result, "USDA: Price No Reason to Avoid Produce," cites a USDA study with some interesting data for us. Luckily, the story is still available on Yahoo!'s site.

Some of the Yahoo! News stories that I attempt to access take me to a Page Not Found error. Yahoo! frequently removes old news stories to make room for new ones. Fret not, however, as another essential feature of Google—Cached pages—saves the day, showing me the page that Google had stored away in its database.

Hopefully, now you feel as if you've gained the knowledge required to get the most out of the Google site.

It's important you don't stop there, however! In the next chapter, we'll cover the plethora of Google services and tools that exist outside of the main Google search site.

You may end up using some of them every day. Indeed, you may wonder how you ever lived without them.

CHAPTER 4

Understanding the Breadth and Depth of Google, Inc.

Google Tools and Services

Google is all about search, but there is more to search than just websites. Google's various online properties encompass resources and tools for searching for and through just about anything electronic, both on- and offline.

These resources can be extremely valuable to marketers and should be considered some of the sharper tools in your research arsenal. This chapter contains a list and basic explanation of Google's tools, along with some useful third-party sites that are Google-powered but not run by Google.

One more thing to note before we get into Google services: Many of them require you to create a Google user account. If you are already signed up for a service like Gmail, then you've already got a Google account. However, once you are logged in, all of Google's services will recognize that—even the ones that don't require a login, like the plain old web search engine. Your search history and click history within search results are also recorded in your Google account. Also, whether or not you are logged into your Google account, the search engine will remember who you are and tune your search results over time so that they match your patterns and preferences.

Table 4-1. Stephan's picks: Top recommended Google-related services

Google Desktop	Program installed on your PC that indexes your documents, emails, and visited web pages. Search from your web browser.
Google Toolbar	Google search within the search results and related functionality integrated into your Internet Explorer or Firefox web browser
Google Pack	Free software for your Windows PC, including antivirus, antispyware, Google Desktop, and much more, all in one easy download
Google Alerts	Automated, free monitoring service of search results in Google and Google News for chosen keywords—a "clipping service" of sorts

Google Books	Google's effort to digitize the world's printed information
Soople	A third-party interface to the Google search engine.
Google Scholar	Search through scholarly literature
Google News	Search and browse news sources (both new and old, worldwide or within a particular country), by news source, relevance, or date
Google Groups	Browse, search, create, and post to discussion groups and Usenet newsgroups and to email discussion lists
Google Images	Search for photos, clipart, logos, icons, and illustrations
Google Directory	A searchable directory of sites, editorially reviewed and organized by topic
Google Search by Country or Language	Search only those websites that are in a particular country
YouTube	Upload, search, and share videos, tag your favorites, and create your own channels
Google+	A powerful new social network from Google. Its features, in Google parlance, include Circles, Huddles, Hangouts, and Sparks.
Google Product Search	Comparison-shopping engine
Blogger	Create a blog for free and host it on Google servers
Google Web History	Remembers your past searches and learns over time, giving you improved search results
Google Blog Search	Allows you to search through an index of RSS feeds
Google Reader	Subscribe to RSS feeds and follow them through this web-based aggregator
Google Q&A	Rather than returning search results, Google sometimes will answer your search query with a factual answer. Built into Google's main search engine.
Google SMS	Search Google by sending your query as a text message through your cell phone and receive the results back as a text message
Google Mobile	Search Google from your web-enabled cell phone or PDA using a pared-down Google web interface designed specifically for mobile devices
Google Talk	Instant messaging software for your computer that supports text chat and voice. Plug in a headset into your PC and talk to your buddies for free over the Internet.
Sidewiki	Read and publish helpful information about any page right in your browser
Google Earth	Software for your PC that allows you to view satellite photos of the earth from space and zoom in.
Picasa	Organize and share your digital photos with this free software that you install on your computer
Google Patent Search	Search through the US Patent and Trademark Office's database of inventions.
Google CSE	The Google Custom Search Engine enables you to harness the power of Google to index and search a network of sites that you specify.
Google Trends	Shows you currently popular search topics, and lets you explore trends in search activity over time for a search term or terms.
Google Insights for Search	Like Google Trends, except you can compare several search terms on a multiline graph.
Google Trends for Websites	Like Google Trends, except it only applies to a network of sites that you specify.

Google Calendar	An online, shareable calendar.
Google Code Search	Search inside of all available open source program code.
Google Mobile App	Transcribes from speech to text, then searches Google from your smartphone.
Google TV	Combines web search, Android apps, and television services in one TV operating environment
Google Voice	A phone number forwarding service
Google Realtime Search	A search engine exclusively for social media.
Google Correlate	Matches search terms with geographic and time-based trend data

Google Desktop

If you are looking for a powerful search application to install on your PC that will search all your Outlook emails, Word documents, Excel spreadsheets, instant messages, previously viewed web pages, and more, then you need go no further than Google's Desktop search tool.

Google Desktop is available to download from *http://desktop.google.com*. It only works on a PC running Windows 7/Vista/XP and Mac OS X 10.4. (For those on newer Macs, Google Quick Search Box is the best way to get Google search functionality outside of a web browser; it's not as good as Google Desktop, but at least it's under active development on the Mac).

It is a simple, painless installation process. After installation, Google Desktop search begins indexing all the files on your hard drive. Quite cleverly, Google integrates Desktop search results along with web search results.

Google Desktop also comes with the Sidebar, a handy little widget that continuously displays on your desktop personalized information such as news headlines, RSS feeds, sticky notes, weather, photos, real-time stock quotes, new email messages, maps, and frequently used files and a quick-find feature that lets you launch programs with a few keystrokes.

Google Toolbar

With the Google Toolbar, you'll always have Google at hand, built into your Internet Explorer or Firefox web browser at the top part of the window. It's a simple process to install and is a small download, available from *http://toolbar.google.com*.

If you choose the option of "Install with Advanced Features" (which I recommend), then you'll be able to see the *PageRank* of any page that you visit. As you may recall, a high PageRank means that Google considers that page important. I tend to think of pages with higher PageRank scores as more trustworthy, although that's not always the case.

This tool is well worth installing, as it eliminates the step of going to Google for every search—which, over time, is a real timesaver.

Google Pack

Available from *http://pack.google.com*, this handy set of applications for Windows XP/Vista/7 includes not just Google Desktop, Google Earth, Picasa, and the Google Toolbar, but other handy tools and utilities such as the RealPlayer media player and Spyware Doctor with Anti-Virus.

Google Alerts

Google will email you the search results (in all manner of results, including Web, news, blogs, realtime, video, and discussions) of your chosen keywords when those results change. Be the first to know when your competitors get some press. Think of it as a "clipping service," except this one is free. Many people configure it to look for their company's name, plus a number of key competitors and similar types of products and services.

This tool is invaluable for researchers and is available at *http://www.google.com/alerts*.

Google Books

Google Books is a massive initiative from Google to digitize a lot of the world's printed information. To use Google Books, go to *http://books.google.com*, or just do an ordinary Google search. When Google finds digitized books with relevant content, those books will be listed along with ordinary Web search results. By clicking on the book title, you can view the page of the book that contains your search terms, as well as other information about the book. You can also display up to two pages before and after the page of the book. Try a web search for *Ecuador trekking* and then click the Google Books link on the left to see this process in action; or search for a famous quote to see which book or books it appears in.

Books have been submitted by more than 20,000 publishers and authors, including Penguin, Wiley, Hyperion, Pearson, Taylor & Francis, Cambridge, Chicago, Oxford, Princeton, and Scholastic.

The advent of Google Books a few years ago marked a monumental shift for Google from being an indexer of the world's knowledge web to a builder of it as well, as noted by industry pundit John Battelle.

Soople

The clever interface at *http://www.soople.com* provides intuitive access to many of Google's more advanced features. You may prefer it over Google's home page. With

Soople, you won't need to remember the query operators to create many of the most useful Google searches.

Google Scholar

Google Scholar, available at *http://scholar.google.com*, allows one to search through scholarly literature including articles from peer reviewed academic journals. Google has worked with publishers to gain access to subscription-only content that wouldn't ordinarily be accessible to search spiders. Although the full content of the article may only be available to subscribers of that journal, Google requires that the publishers provide at least abstracts to Google Scholar searchers.

Search results displayed in Google Scholar each have a "cited by" link which, when clicked on, will show you all the citations to that document in the scholarly literature that Google Scholar knows about.

Google News

You've already learned how to search Google News. I have only a couple of things I would like to add to what I covered there. First, you should get to know the Advanced Search page on Google News at *http://news.google.com/news/advanced_news_search*. It's a helpful tool to narrow a search by location, by news source, by date range, and so on.

Second, if you consider yourself a news junkie, you may want to make the Google News home page, at *http://news.google.com*, or the Google News business page, at *http://news .google.com/news?topic=b*, your "start page" that opens up when you start your web browser. It's a great way to keep up with current events. You can also use iGoogle for further customization of a Google-based personal home page.

Groups

This link will take you to the Google Groups search engine, which searches discussion groups on Google Groups as well as millions of Usenet newsgroup messages dating back to 1981. Usenet is a part of the Internet dedicated to online discussion, and these discussion groups/forums (known as newsgroups) number in the tens of thousands. Type in your search query, then click the Groups link in the More menu at the top of the search page to jump directly to Google Groups results.

Google Groups will also allow you to create, join and search email-based mailing lists, including restricted lists. In addition, you have the ability to track and mark favorite topics using the "My Groups" feature.

If you want to get the "dirt" and hear what people are saying in Usenet and email discussion forums about your company, a competitor, or an industry, Google Groups is a great resource.

Google Images

The Advanced Image Search page at *http://images.google.com/advanced_image _search*, which allows you to refine your search by size, coloration, file type, and more is quite useful. If you don't want to permanently set your image settings, or if you want to adjust a query that has already been executed, you can use a parameter to restrict the results of a single query:

- &imgtype=face
- &imgtype=news
- &imgtype=photo
- &imgtype=clipart
- &imgtype=lineart

You can also click the Similar Images link below the results in a Google Images search to see results that Google has determined are similar, or you can upload your own photo and search for similar ones.

Google Search by Country or Language

Google allows you to search solely within those websites that are located in a specific country or written in a specific language. Google also offers search sites at each of the major country domains (Google France, Google Germany, Google UK, Google Australia, Google Canada, etc.).

Each Google country site has a radio button to restrict search results to pages within that country, in which case the site must be hosted within that country or have that country's domain extension. A comprehensive list is available at *http://www.google .com/language_tools*.

YouTube

The ubiquitous YouTube, at *http://www.youtube.com*, is a Google property and is by far the most popular site on the Web for sharing and finding video clips of all types. You can create your own "channel" and subscribe to other channels as well. It's a great resource for easily finding news video, movie trailers and clips, live performances, helpful how-to tutorials, and much more.

Google+ (Google Plus)

This new social network holds a lot of promise. Whether it will be the Facebook-killer that Google employees are hoping for or a flop like Google Wave was is still to be determined. Group your friends into Circles, set up customized news feeds (known as Sparks), have Huddles (group chats), and make yourself available for impromptu meetups (in Hangouts), among other things. Expect ever deeper integration of Google + with an array of Google products, including Gmail, Chrome, Chat, and, of course, Google web search.

Google Product Search

http://www.google.com/prdhp

Formerly known as Froogle, this service searches through ecommerce sites and indexes their product listings. There's a more detailed explanation of Google Product Search earlier in this book.

Blogger

Google's blogging service is available at *http://www.blogger.com*. Blogger offers free blog hosting, templates and remote blogging software. If you wish, you can also host your blog on your own domain.

Google Web History

Wouldn't it be cool if your search engine got smarter the more you used it? That is what Google Web History hopes to achieve. By analyzing your past searches, it hopes to give more targeted and relevant results to you in the future. You can use this on multiple computers. All you have to do is just be logged into your Google account on your computer and it will track your past searches, show you what your searches were so you can conduct them again, and also show you what you clicked on in the past. You can view your saved web history at *http://www.google.com/searchhistory*.

Google Blog Search

This blog-specific search engine, found at http://blogsearch.google.com, is actually a search engine of RSS feeds rather than blogs. More specifically, blogs without RSS feeds won't make it into Google Blog Search. However, sites that aren't blogs but have RSS feeds are included. If your blog is not listed, you can submit your RSS feed here: *http://blogsearch.google.com*

With the advanced search functionality in Google Blog Search, you can search by author, by date range, and by blog.

Google Reader

A web-based RSS feed aggregator to compete with services such as My Yahoo!, My MSN, and Bloglines. It's well worth checking out, particularly if you prefer subscribing to RSS feeds through a website, rather than an installed application on your computer. Available at *http://reader.google.com*.

Google Q&A

This isn't actually a separate service; it's built right into the Google search interface. Sometimes when you submit a query to Google, in addition to returning the standard sort of search results, Google may provide you with a direct answer to your question, also citing (and linking to) the source that it obtained the answer from. You may see these answers at the top of the results page, or even at the top of the list of suggested queries that pop up underneath your typing.

For example, either the query *when was Einstein born?* or an equivalent query of *Einstein birthday* will return the date of his birth at the top of the search results. Here are some more example queries that return Google Q&A results: *President of France, what is the birthplace of Bono?, square root of 2, capital of Canada,* and *height of Mt. Everest.* Microsoft considers this same capability a major feature of Bing, which they call a "decision engine" instead of a "search engine."

Google SMS

On the go with just an SMS-capable cell phone in your pocket? No problem! Just conduct your search from your cell phone by sending Google your query as an SMS text message to the US shortcode 466453 (GOOGLE on most phones). You'll then receive one or more text messages back with your results, usually within a minute. Results may be labeled as "1/3", "2/3", and so on. To get Google SMS help info sent directly to your phone, send the word 'help' as a text message to 466453. Or learn more at *http://sms .google.com.*

Google Mobile

If you have a web-connected cell phone, smartphone, or handheld device, you can search Google using a pared-down interface designed specifically for mobile devices. Just enter in *http://www.google.com* (or *http://www.google.com/xhtml* if you get an error) and you're on your way! Learn more at *http://www.google.com/mobile.*

Google Talk

Google has its own messenger software dubbed Google Talk to compete with instant messaging software such as ICQ, AOL Instant Messenger, MSN Messenger or Yahoo! Messenger. It supports not just text message chat, but also voice over the Internet (like Skype and Apple's iChat). In other words, you can converse for free with any other Google Talk user by using a headset or microphone. Download Google Talk from *http: //talk.google.com.* You'll also find links there for a voice and video chat plug-in that lets you use a webcam for video chatting in Gmail or iGoogle.

Sidewiki

Google Sidewiki is an annotations feature of the Google Toolbar that adds a browser sidebar, where users can add and read comments for the browser's current web page. This means you can get other's opinions about a news story, product reviews and other comments which the site owner can't control or delete. You may find this helpful for getting further information about a site or its content where user comments are not allowed or are heavily edited. Learn more about Google Sidewiki at *http://www.google .com/sidewiki*.

Google Earth

This software that installs on your PC or Mac allows you to see satellite views of any-where on the Earth from space, along with street maps (available for all of the United States and many other countries) overlaid with optional views. Point and click, and satellite images and local facts zoom into view. You can tilt and rotate the view to check out the terrain and buildings. Obtain driving directions and "fly" along your route. You can zoom in from space right into your neighborhood. You can download Google Earth at *http://earth.google.com*.

Picasa

Another one of Google's acquisitions, Picasa was a digital photo management com-pany. Google offers the full-featured Picasa digital photo management software as a free download, at *http://picasa.google.com*. The software allows you to easily organize and share your digital photographs, write captions for your pics, order prints, apply color corrections and other photo effects, and even make gift CDs and online photo albums for friends and family.

Google Patent Search

http://www.google.com/patents

This service enables you to search through the USPTO archives of over 7 million patents to look for registered and pending patents. It's particularly helpful for entrepreneurs and people who are marketing new inventions.

Google CSE (Custom Search Engine)

http://www.google.com/cse

Rather than develop your own search engine or integrate bulky search source code libraries and maintain your own index, why not outsource it all to Google? Just select the sites for which you want to create a private index, then paste in the code snippet where you want the search box to appear. Google CSE includes some nice features like on-demand indexing and autocompletion of the query.

Google Trends

http://www.google.com/trends

Google Trends is an extremely useful tool for keyword research, especially if your sites deal in seasonal or trend-conscious merchandise. The initial page shows currently popular topics and searches, but you can also search for a particular term or terms and get extra information about the search popularity of those terms over time. This includes line graphs of search activity and links to related pages.

Google Insights for Search

http://www.google.com/insights/search

Google Insights for Search allows you to compare keyword trends across multiple categories, sites, markets, and even time ranges. It can show things like regional interest in different terms, related searches that are rising in popularity, trend forecasts, and more. Additional features are available if you're signed in to your Google account.

Google Trends for Websites

http://trends.google.com/websites/

This service works just like Google Trends, except you can tune it for your own site or network of sites to determine what your visitors or users are searching for.

Google Calendar

http://www.google.com/calendar

While not particularly useful for market research, Google Calendar is an extremely useful tool. It relieves you of the responsibility of maintaining persistent scheduling and appointment data over multiple machines. It syncs your iPhone or Android phone with your laptop so it's easy to see your appointments when you're on the go.

Google Code Search

http://www.google.com/codesearch

This service enables you to search inside of all available open source program code. You can refine the results by language, license, and package format.

Google Mobile App for Smartphones

http://www.google.com/mobile

Or, on your smartphone:

http://m.google.com

The Google Mobile App offers a variety of features to enhance your smartphone browsing experience. The Search by Voice application transcribes from speech to text, then searches Google from your iPhone, Blackberry, Android, or other smartphone.

Google TV

http://www.google.com/tv

Google TV is an open source platform for web-enabled televisions and third-party web-connected devices that combines web search with regular cable and satellite TV services. Since Google TV is based on Android, many existing Android apps will work through it, and you can even use your Android phone as a remote control for a Google TV-enabled device.

Google Voice

http://www.google.com/voice/

Google Voice is a phone number forwarding service, though it has many interesting features beyond just relaying one number to another. To begin with, you can create a new number to forward to several other numbers, or you can use one of your existing numbers as the Google Voice number. You can create intricate rules that forward to different phones at different times of day, or block certain callers, or have Google transcribe your voice mail, and a variety of other telephony services.

Google Realtime Search

Realtime Search used to index social media sites like Twitter and Facebook, but currently it only works through a Google+ search. If you're logged into Google+ and search for something in the Google+ window, you'll see an option for "X more recent posts" near the top of the search results. If you click this link, you'll turn on realtime search throughout Google+, enabling you to see new results as they become available.

Google may reconnect the other services that it used to index for Realtime Search someday. In the meantime, all other social media content is available through a normal Web search.

Google Correlate

http://www.google.com/trends/correlate

This service combines search terms with their popularity over time or throughout different regions. This enables you to search for information within the context of a time period, season, or geographic region.

Applying Google's Tools

It's time to resurrect our hypothetical research task, where we aimed to find market research relating to the frozen vegetable industry.

How might the tools we just reviewed help us gain the information we seek? Consider these steps:

Let's start with Google Books. A competitor search for *"birds eye" -view vegetables "green giant"* returns books on dieting and cooking.

With Google Personalized Search enabled, search for *birds eye –view* and see what comes back; this exercise will be slightly different for everyone, depending on how much data Google has collected on your search habits.

In Google Groups, search for *organic frozen vegetables*, then take note of the debates among consumers on the pros and cons of frozen vegetables.

A search on Google Scholar for frozen vegetables turns up studies on the effects of freezing a vegetable, along with information on market demand for vegetables, and methods of detecting microbial infections on frozen vegetables, some of which is useful data for this research project.

Making Your Desktop More Efficient

Organization consultants usually start at their client's desk. I advise, however, to start with your PC's desktop. Arrange your virtual office environment for maximum productivity in online researching, as follows:

Install the Google Pack and Google Toolbar, with enhanced features enabled.

Sign up for Google Reader and select some of your favorite blogs and news sites to subscribe to their RSS feeds. Be sure to include feeds from Research Buzz (*http://Re searchBuzz.org*), The Shifted Librarian (*http://TheShiftedLibrarian.com*), Google Blogoscoped (*http://blogoscoped.com*), Search Engine Land (*http://searchengineland.com*), my blog where I frequently comment on search marketing (*http://StephanSpencer .com*), the Official Google Blog (*http://googleblog.blogspot.com*), and *http://Marketing Profs.com*.

Load up your key competitor's names, your company and brand names, etc. into Google Alerts.

Set your browser start page to something more useful like your iGoogle page, Google Reader, Google News, etc.

Buy a reference book on Google for your bookshelf, such as *The Art of SEO*.

Create a cheat sheet of the query operators you most want to start using, print it, and keep it near your computer.

Configure your Google Toolbar to include other search types that you might frequently use, such as Craigslist or Wikipedia. You can manage these from the dropdown on the right of the Search button on the Google Toolbar.

CHAPTER 5

Forming a Good Research Strategy

According to an IDC (International Data Corporation) report, knowledge workers spend 15–30% of their day searching for information. What's worse, more than half of their online searches fail.

This book has certainly helped you to increase your odds of search success. The focus of this chapter is to examine how some Google experts—Tasha Bergson-Michelson, Philipp Lenssen, Nancy Blachman, and Tara Calishain—form their successful search strategies.

Tasha Bergson-Michelson is a Search Education Curriculum Fellow (*https://sites.google.com/site/gwebsearcheducation*) at Google, Inc.

Philipp Lenssen is author of *Google Apps Hacks* (O'Reilly 2008) and publishes the *Blogoscoped* website (*http://www.blogoscoped.com*).

Nancy Blachman is coauthor of *How To Do Everything With Google* (McGraw Hill 2003) and publishes the *Google Guide* e-book and website (*http://www.googleguide.com*).

Tara Calishain is author of the *Web Search Garage* (Prentice Hall 2004) and *Information Trapping: Real-Time Research on the Web* (New Riders Press 2006), coauthor of *Google Hacks, 3rd ed.* (O'Reilly 2009), and publishes the *ResearchBuzz website* (*http://www.ResearchBuzz.org*).

Choosing the Right Tool for the Job

In the interviews throughout this chapter, the above-mentioned experts explain some of their advanced search tactics and strategies.

Stephan: Since your specialty is search education, Tasha, are there any training resources that you'd particularly recommend to anyone wanting to become an expert Google searcher?

Tasha: If your participants want to practice search regularly, they can check out AGoogleADay.com, a daily search challenge that runs in the NYT every day above the crossword puzzle. They can also go directly to *http://www .agoogleaday.com* to play.

Stephan: For what sort of research tasks is a major search engine not well suited?

Nancy: The UC Berkeley Library has a wonderful chart for suggesting when to use a search engine, subject directory, specialized database, or an expert. It's part of their "Finding Information on the Internet" tutorial (*http://www.lib .berkeley.edu/TeachingLib/Guides/Internet/Strategies.html*).

Tara: Stuff like these interview questions! Mostly questions where you want to ask an expert several things, where you want to "pick someone's brain." Thankfully, the Internet can help you FIND the experts. If you have a situation where you need to explore only known and credible information, then you might want to use a paid search engine like LexNex or the friendly experts at your local library. You might be able to find what you need via a general search engine, but you'd have to use a subscription service to actually get to it.

Philipp: I think a search engine can be part of any research, with three caveats.

First, you need to know how to appropriately evaluate the trust for a given page you stumble upon, as well for a given area of research. Any page you stumble upon in Google or others needs to be evaluated based on many criteria—a science on its own, parts of which become intuition after some time. Beyond that, there are areas of research where you need to be especially careful; like when you want to verify if a popular myth holds any truth, such as a quotation being attributed to someone, an anecdote relating to a famous person, an urban legend, or a "truth" where a lobbying group or popular political party has an interest in it. With areas like these, even finding a dozen repetitions of that "truth" may not be enough for you to gain appropriate trust in it.

Second, researching in areas where you lack the specific words to describe the idea. In the age of Google, a keyword is also literally a key: without the key, the door remains locked. Imagine you would want to find the name of a painter of a given painting you came across a year ago. The mainstream search engines of today won't let you take a pencil and draw what little you may remember of the painting, to then return similar images to you. There are some interesting developments in this area—I'm a big fan of *http:// TinEye.com*, which lets you upload an image to find similar likely ones, and there are also search engines which let you whistle to find songs—but mostly, things are still keyword based. Third, there are certain characters which Google and others ignore. For instance, Microsoft once released a programming language called C# (pronounced c-sharp). There are already other programming languages called C and C++. But how do you separate these languages in Google, when Google usually ignores characters like "#" or "+"?

Added to these, there's the challenge of being confronted with powers that be which may, every once in a while, work to make your research harder. It's a more philosophical topic and not just a problem when using search engines. The basic communication approach of the powers is to hide, re-define, and distract. Let's say John Doe is the leader of Doetonia, and he just got bribed with a big black suitcase filled with a billion Doetonia dollars. In utopia, informed citizens would be all over the place entering words like "john doe suitcase scandal" into the Google of their land. In the reality of our hypothetical example however, first of all, the scandal may not be known or if it's known, it will be almost not covered (hiding!). Second, if the incident becomes known, the Doetonia press agency as well as other press houses which have an interest in the established system remaining stable can start to call it the "gentleman's lapse of reason incident" or so, making it sound much more harmless—research this topic now using those words, and you may find some pros and cons in regards to the incident, but basically be stuck in a world defined by the Doe-establishment, because you've already started to use their words (redefining!). Third, if the incident becomes known and just reframing the issue won't suffice, the Doe team and like-minded press can now create a red herring controversy in another area. Maybe they've just discovered that the pet cat of Ms. Doe has died in a car accident because there was no fence around the Doetonia leader house, and this becomes the discussion of the day, and all Doetonians jump to search engines to research the name of the cat, or whether the country should make fences mandatory for every citizen owning a pet cat (distraction!).

Stephan: For what sort of research tasks is Google not well suited, but another major search engine is? Which search engine(s) do you turn to in such occasions?

Nancy: Good question. I came across this page, *http://www.bcps.org/offices/lis/models/tips/searching.html*, that lists when to use which search engine. You can also find charts listing features of the most popular search engines, e.g. *http://www.infopeople.org/search/chart.html*.

Tara: Searchable Subject Indexes (Yahoo!, DMOZ) are best for finding general topics—famous people, or topics you can't narrow down much. Search for George Washington in Yahoo! and in Google and note the differences in the kind of results you get.

Philipp: *http://TinEye.com* as mentioned above is one. Knowing a couple of specialized search engines might be helpful for sure, but sometimes Google also releases a specialized search engine of their own which is superior to the original. Take Google Patent Search, which was much more accessible than the official US government's patent search. The official government search site oddly enough uses images saved in a non-web compatible format, so you'll have trouble looking at the patent illustrations at their site!

One research tool I can highly recommend isn't really a tool at all—it's paid Q&A site *http://Uclue.com*. You set your price, ask a question, and have one of the researchers get back to you. The Uclue researchers were formerly working at Google Answers, before that got shut down.

Stephan: What are your favorite Google query operators, and why?

Nancy: **define:** Shows definitions from pages on the Web. For example, *define:blog* will show definitions for "Blog" (weB LOG).

filetype: Restrict the results to pages whose names end with the specified suffix. For example, *interviewing salary negotiation filetype:pdf* restricts results to pdf documents with tips on job interviewing and salary negotiation.

allintitle: Restrict results to those containing all the query terms you specify in the title. For example, find a link to the wonderful widely circulated well-written fantasy "commencement speech" purportedly given by Kurt Vonnegut at MIT. The imaginary speech began "Wear sunscreen," so you can find it with the query *allintitle: wear sunscreen*.

site: Restrict your search results to the site or domain you specify. For example, find every page on a site that's included in Google's index with a query like *site:www.googleguide.com*.

location: Restrict your query on Google news to only articles from the location specified. For example, to find news about John Kerry in one of the contested states, use *location:OH "John Kerry"*.

Tara: **site:** Helps me narrow down search a lot.

intitle: You know a page is focused on a topic when the topic word is in the title.

Philipp: Google has become fuzzier over the years, meaning they more frequently ignore certain words or automatically list results they consider to be targeting the word "you really meant." But sometimes, you might have actually meant what you've originally written. In these cases, the quotation mark search operator comes in handy again.

One operator I use a lot is *site:example.com foobar*, where example.com is the site you want to search across, and "foobar" is the keyword. You can even throw *intitle:something* into this mix to restrict it to sites from example.com which have the word "something" in their page title... perhaps because such pages are of a different type, and you only want to find that type. Say, *intitle:buy-this-product*. Note that the site operator also works with subdirectories, so *site:example.com/archive/2009/* is an option, too.

Stephan: Besides www.google.com (*http://www.google.com*), what are your favorite Google-owned websites, and why?

Tasha: I just cannot get enough of filtering by color in the left-hand panel in Google Images. Here are some of my favorite use-cases:

> Some people love searching *tesla* and seeing that red skews towards car, while purple skews towards the coils themselves. I love how for *tesla coil*, a plain image search mostly brings back images of a tesla coil, but clicking on the white filter tends towards diagrams about tesla coils.
>
> When I was in Kenya, and was looking for pictures of the national football team, the Harambee Stars, I got lots of pictures of them standing in lines for team photos, but I wanted them playing. What is the difference with a team playing? You see lots of the field in between players, which is green. So I click on the green filter, and go from static portraits to actions shots. The same works with *sf giants*, to move from logos to action shots.
>
> All-time favorite: How often do you read a book, and later only remember the topic and a vague memory of the cover? So, you were talking to your kids about the great Wangari Maathai on the event of her passing, and wanted to find that kids' book where she was wearing a turquoise dress? Search *wangari maathai book*, click on turquoise, and it should pop right up. Google Images does not necessarily have cover shots of every book, but it sure is a help to me.

Tara: I like Google News (*http://news.google.com*); I use it a lot. It's got a great list of sources and now you can search by a date range.

Philipp: I use Gmail a lot. When I'm in countries where YouTube is accessible, I use that a lot (though at the moment I'm living in China, where I can't access it). Other Google tools like Google Image Search and Google Maps are very useful, too. Google Images can search by color, search for faces only and more. You can also use the *site:* operator, as described earlier, in conjunction with a Google Image search.

Stephan: What are your favorite third-party applications that are based on Google?

Nancy: *Google Alert*
> *http://www.google.com/alerts*

Fagan Finder's Translation Wizard
> *http://www.faganfinder.com/translate/*

Fagan Finder's Search Tool
> *http://www.faganfinder.com*

Soople
> *http://www.soople.com*

Search result evaluation checklist
> *http://www.lib.berkeley.edu/TeachingLib/Guides/Internet/EvalForm.pdf*

Philipp: Google's search and translation APIs are nice. You can write interesting tools on top of that. I recently looked into writing a text editor based on JavaScript, which would run locally inside the browser but still be able to open files (you can google for *"Netpadd B"* to see what I came up with). In that plain text editor, you can mark any piece of text, hit a certain shortcut, and a translation of that text into English will pop up. (Or, if the text is English to begin with, it will be translated into Chinese.) There are many interesting tools and sites out there making use of Google's APIs and gadgets.

A Market Research Scavenger Hunt

I enlisted our guru Nancy to formulate search queries on a hunt for market research information for two industries—bed & breakfasts and online car buying. The exercise was merely to gain an insight into her search term strategies.

Stephan: What Google search query would you use if you were looking for a list of the most popular guidebooks of B&Bs in the United States?

Nancy: *"bed * breakfasts" OR "b&b" "U.S." OR "United States" OR USA*

Stephan: What search query would you use if you were looking for the number of bed and breakfasts in the United States?

Nancy: This is the search I suggest: *"bed * breakfasts in u.s."*

Stephan: What search query would you use if you were looking for the amount of money that bed and breakfasts in the United States spend per year on marketing?

Nancy: *"bed * breakfasts in u.s."*

Stephan: What search query would you use if you were looking for the number of new cars purchased annually over the Internet in the United States?

Nancy: *new cars purchased Internet in the "United States" OR "US" OR USA*

Stephan: What search query would you use if you were looking for a list of the top few biggest sellers of new cars over the Internet by sales volume?

Nancy: *sales cars purchased over the internet*

revenue cars purchased over the internet

Stephan: What would your search query be if you were looking for a fairly comprehensive market research report for a business plan of a virtual dealership of new cars that supports online purchase? (paid reports are fine; it doesn't have to be free.)

Nancy: *market research cars purchased over the internet*

The Path to Google Greatness

Stephan: How does one assess the quality or credibility of the information produced by the search and various sources? Any practical tips beyond the obvious "buyer beware" type of advice?

Nancy: Google's web page ranking system, PageRank, tends to give priority to better respected and trusted information. Well-respected sites link to other well-respected sites. This linking boosts the PageRank of high-quality sites. Consequently, more accurate pages are typically listed before sites that include unreliable and erroneous material. Nevertheless, evaluate carefully whatever you find on the Web since anyone can:

- Create pages
- Exchange ideas
- Copy, falsify or omit information intentionally or accidentally

Many people publish pages to get you to buy something or accept a point of view. Google makes no effort to discover or eliminate unreliable and erroneous material. It's up to you to cultivate the habit of healthy skepticism. When evaluating the credibility of a page, consider the following AAOCC (Authority, Accuracy, Objectivity, Currency, Coverage) criteria and questions, which are adapted from *http://www.lib.berkeley.edu/scien ces/guides/how_to_evaluate_electronic_resources*

Authority:

- Who are the authors? Are they qualified? Are they credible?
- With whom are they affiliated? Do their affiliations affect their credibility?
- Who is the publisher? What is the publisher's reputation?

Accuracy:

- Is the information accurate? Is it reliable and error-free?
- Are the interpretations and implications reasonable?
- Is there evidence to support conclusions? Is the evidence verifiable?
- Do the authors properly list their sources, references or citations with dates, page numbers or web addresses, etc.?

Objectivity:

- What is the purpose? What do the authors want to accomplish?
- Does this purpose affect the presentation?
- Is there an implicit or explicit bias?
- Is the information fact, opinion, spoof, or satirical?

Currency:

- Is the information current? Is it still valid?
- When was the site last updated?
- Is the site well maintained? Are there any broken links?

Coverage:

- Is the information relevant to your topic and assignment?
- What is the intended audience?
- Is the material presented at an appropriate level?
- Is the information complete? Is it unique?

Search for *evaluate web pages* or *hints evaluate credibility web pages* to find resources on how to evaluate the veracity of pages you view.

For a printable form with most of the questions that you will probably want to ask, visit *http://www.lib.berkeley.edu/TeachingLib/Guides/Internet/Eval Form.pdf*. For more information on evaluating what you find, visit *http://www.lib.berkeley.edu/TeachingLib/Guides/Internet/Evaluate.html*.

Tara: I give sites more credibility when they have their own domain (versus being set up on a free hosting site). I give more credibility when a site is updated regularly—and by regularly I don't mean once a year or so. I like having some kind of "about this page" set up on the site. I like when content updates are dated. I like when sites fully source some of their claims. Of course there are exceptions to rules, there's great content set up on free websites, but these are my rules of thumb. And it also helps to have a really good BS detector.

Philipp: A huge number of details are involved. For instance:

- Does the article or page contain a full author name? Does it contain a date?
- Does the author have an About page, perhaps even with picture and full address?
- Can I verify that the author is who he claims he is? Do I know the domain, can I trust it?
- What does the design look like?
- What's the page's PageRank? Not that there's no scams on Page Rank-5 sites or so, but usually, I would trust a PR7 page more than a PR0 page, simply because apparently it was around for some time and got linked. You just need to make sure this won't be your only indicator of trust, because some scammers may know how to optimize their PageRank. It's just part of the mixture of signals.
- How commercial is the field I'm moving into? Conversely, how much of a hobby effort is it? Instinctively, I think hobby efforts with a very

small target group are less likely to be a scam. "Cool screensaver" would be a topic where I'd be very, very careful. "Peter's postage stamp archiving program", I might be more likely to install, if I find that I get to know Peter on his page and he seems to care about the subject.

- An .edu domain may emit some extra trust, but again, you need to be careful to not take any single parameter on its own.

- Is the article well-researched? Spellchecked? Are the ads surrounding it sensible, or just too much?

- Is there a conflict of interest at play? Am I being sold a product?

- Can I confirm the found data from other sources?

Stephan: What one piece of advice about using Google as a research tool should the reader retain, if they remember nothing else?

Nancy: You can find quite a bit of information using Google. However, not all information on the Web is available through Google. If you don't find what you want by using Google, try another search tool or service.

Philipp: Sometimes, using a particular word may be necessary to find the right set of pages, even if that word may be synonymous to what you've already searched for. Try to imagine how an author of your imaginary ideal target page might phrase their sentences. Perhaps, when describing that baroque painting you vaguely remember and of which you forgot the artist name, you would need to write *voluptuous lady* instead of *overweight woman* to find the right result.

CHAPTER 6

The Technical Side of Web Research

This last chapter is specifically for search engine optimization (SEO) practitioners and web developers who are looking for an edge when it comes to advanced Google skills. This sort of information changes rapidly due to the perpetual motion of search engine development and the desire for Google engineers to avoid being too helpful to black hat SEOs, so soak it all up and check the next edition of this book for updated tips and tricks.

SEO for Firefox

Before you do anything else, update your Firefox browser to the latest release, then download and install the SEO for Firefox plug-in:

> *http://tools.seobook.com/firefox/seo-for-firefox.html*

This plug-in transforms your browser into an outstanding research tool that will help you determine how sites in Google SERPs rank in a variety of relevant search engines and social media sites.

Advanced Query String Parameters

Most of the operators listed above should suffice for most searches. However, if you really need to get extra specific, here's the hidden stash. All parameters are set using the = operator and assume a base URL of:

> *http://www.google.com/search?*

Separate multiple parameters with the ampersand (&) character.

Table 6-1. Google query parameters

Query parameter	Description
q	The search query; can also be typed out in long form as "query"
as_epq	Matches an exact phrase, same effect as using quotes around words

Query parameter	Description
as_oq	Matches at least one term, same effect as the OR operator
as_eq	Excludes this term, same effect as the - operator
as_occt	Restrict results to those where the query occurs only in title, body, url, or links
as_filetype	Returns results that match the specified three-letter filetype extension
as_ft	Includes or excludes files with the filetype specified with as_filetype, options are i and e for include or exclude
sitesearch	Has the same effect as the site: operator
as_sitesearch	Like sitesearch, but shows site:URL in the search box, can be used together with as_dt
as_dt	Use this with as_sitesearch to return results from a specific URL(the i switch), or from all except that URL (the e switch)
as_rq	Returns sites related to the specified URL, same effect as the related: operator
as_lq	Returns all sites linking to the specified URL, same effect as the link: operator
hl	Specifies the language used in the Google interface
lr	Language restrict. Uses standard two-letter language codes
ie	Input encoding
oe	Output encoding
safe	Toggles Google's safe search filtering. Values are active and off
tbs	Restrict results to the given time interval, where the time is qdr:(range). For the range, use y for year, m for month, w for week, d for day, h for hour, n for minute, and s for second (without the parentheses). You can also follow each one with an optional number, e.g. npr=qdr:d4 to get results indexed in the last 4 days.

Adding Omitted Results

Under most circumstances, you're primarily concerned with the first SERP, and maybe the second page, but only if you're on it. What if you want to see the end of the list, though? Seeing the bottom ten results is more difficult than it sounds at first. Fortunately, there are some query parameters you can use to go to the last page of results and add omitted results. This also gives a more accurate estimated count of total results than Google's initial estimate:

> &filter=0&start=990

Just append that to your query string and press Enter (Google Instant must be disabled in order for this to work).

Finding People to Link to You

It can be very difficult to find people who are willing to link to your pages, especially if your primary method is cold-emailing. If you can narrow the list of targets to include only sites that are topic-appropriate, where a link to your page won't seem out of place or unusual, you've got an edge. So how do you do that? With Google search operators, of course! By using the *site:* operator in Google, for instance:

*site:edu | site:gov [some industry] "website * by" | "email * by"*

In the above example, we're limiting results to educational and government sites that have content related to a certain unspecified industry, and looking for contact information (government and academic top-level domains are trusted, authoritative and important in the eyes of Google, since .gov and .edu links tend to be in more pristine link neighborhoods). This will return a more focused result set that will result in high quality links.

Reducing the Result Set When Testing For Indexation

Google won't let you go beyond the 1000th result, so if you are checking a site to see how well it is indexed (e.g. checking a competitor's website), you're going to run into that limit if the site has more than 1000 pages. In these situations, you can work around the limit by looking at just a subset of the site by using the *site:* and *inurl:* operators. For example, this will return only the results found in the articles directory of this site:

site:www.example.com/articles/

But what if you have more than 1000 pages in that directory? You use the *inurl:* operator to return a more limited result set:

site:www.example.com/articles/ inurl:january

That should return all of the articles with "january" in the file name. Hopefully you've employed a naming convention that will allow you to follow this procedure. If not, you may have to get creative with some other operators, such as *intext:* and *filetype:*.

Monitoring Incoming Links and Measuring Anchor Text Strength

Incoming link text is extremely important for determining which search terms your pages end up being associated with. Google will tell you what pages it associates with any given link text when you use the *allinanchor:* and *inanchor:* operators. So if you want to see who is linking to a page that sells frozen vegetables, you might use this query:

allinanchor: frozen vegetables

That will probably return a lot of results. Some of them may be interesting, but perhaps you're more interested in seeing how people really feel about your products:

allinanchor: worst | rotten | gross | disgusting frozen vegetables

Hopefully your page isn't in that SERP! If it is, you might consider contacting the blogger or webmaster responsible for that page and asking him what you can do to solve the problem.

The allinanchor: operator, used in a similar fashion to the above examples, can also be good for checking the strength of anchor text. Your keywords may not match up to your anchor text; if this is the case, you may need to do some fine-tuning of various aspects of site design, ad campaigns, and overall marketing once your keyword and anchor text research are completed.

Checking Image Indexing

Depending on the kind of business you're running, you may or may not want certain images from your site to be indexed. In most cases, product images that link back to your site are a good thing because people who search for those products in Google Images may click your photos and get to your pages. On the other hand, you may not want photos from the company holiday party to be the top result for brand and product searches, so you may want to remove them.

The way to check image indexing is by using the site: operator in Google Images:

site:example.com

This query, when modified for your domain name and executed from the search box on *http://images.google.com*, will show all of the images that Google has indexed from your site.

About the Author

Stephan M. Spencer, M.Sc., is an author of *The Art of SEO*, published in October 2009 by O'Reilly and coauthored by Eric Enge, Rand Fishkin, and Jessie Stricchiola.

Stephan is the founder of Netconcepts. Netconcepts started out as a web design and marketing agency, but over time morphed into a leading SEO firm. Stephan, and Netconcepts, had been heavy into the science of SEO since 1999.

Netconcepts was acquired in January 2010 by paid and organic search software/services agency Covario. Covario is one of the rare companies to make it onto the Inc. 500 list two years in a row—in 2009 and again in 2010.

Stephan is the inventor of the automated pay-for-performance natural search technology platform GravityStream, now rebranded as Covario's Organic Search Optimizer.

Stephan is a Senior Contributor to Practical Ecommerce and to MarketingProfs.com, a monthly columnist on Search Engine Land, and a regular contributor to Multichannel Merchant magazine. He's also contributed to DM News, Catalog Age, Catalog Success, Unlimited, and NZ Marketing magazine, among others.

He is a frequent conference speaker on SEO and other online marketing topics for the Direct Marketing Association (DMA), American Marketing Association (AMA), Shop.org, Internet Retailer, SMX, IncisiveMedia (Search Engine Strategies), O'Reilly/TechWeb, PubCon, ECMOD, IQPC, and IIR. His many hundreds of speaking gigs have taken him around the globe—everywhere from Berlin, London, Toronto, Santiago, and Auckland to New York, Chicago, San Francisco, Los Angeles, and places in between.

Stephan is an avid blogger. He blogs primarily on his own blog, Stephan Spencer's Scatterings. But his posts can also be found on Searchlight (part of the CNET Blog Network), Shop.org Blog, Natural Search Blog, BusinessBlogConsulting.com, MarketingProfs Daily Fix, Changes For Good, and Google, I Suggest.

Stephan can be contacted via email at *stephan@stephanspencer.com* or by phone at (608) 209-2595.

Colophon

The animal on the cover of *Google Power Search* is a chanting falcon.

The cover image is from *Wood's Animate Creations*. The cover font is Adobe ITC Garamond. The text font is Linotype Birka; the heading font is Adobe Myriad Condensed; and the code font is LucasFont's TheSansMonoCondensed.

Get even more for your money.

Join the O'Reilly Community, and register the O'Reilly books you own. It's free, and you'll get:

- $4.99 ebook upgrade offer
- 40% upgrade offer on O'Reilly print books
- Membership discounts on books and events
- Free lifetime updates to ebooks and videos
- Multiple ebook formats, DRM FREE
- Participation in the O'Reilly community
- Newsletters
- Account management
- 100% Satisfaction Guarantee

Signing up is easy:

1. Go to: oreilly.com/go/register
2. Create an O'Reilly login.
3. Provide your address.
4. Register your books.

Note: English-language books only

To order books online:
oreilly.com/store

For questions about products or an order:
orders@oreilly.com

To sign up to get topic-specific email announcements and/or news about upcoming books, conferences, special offers, and new technologies:
elists@oreilly.com

For technical questions about book content:
booktech@oreilly.com

To submit new book proposals to our editors:
proposals@oreilly.com

O'Reilly books are available in multiple DRM-free ebook formats. For more information:
oreilly.com/ebooks

O'REILLY®

Spreading the knowledge of innovators   oreilly.com

The information you need, when and where you need it.

With Safari Books Online, you can:

Access the contents of thousands of technology and business books

- Quickly search over 7000 books and certification guides
- Download whole books or chapters in PDF format, at no extra cost, to print or read on the go
- Copy and paste code
- Save up to 35% on O'Reilly print books
- **New!** Access mobile-friendly books directly from cell phones and mobile devices

Stay up-to-date on emerging topics before the books are published

- Get on-demand access to evolving manuscripts.
- Interact directly with authors of upcoming books

Explore thousands of hours of video on technology and design topics

- Learn from expert video tutorials
- Watch and replay recorded conference sessions

Spreading the knowledge of innovators   safari.oreilly.com

CPSIA information can be obtained at www.ICGtesting.com
Printed in the USA
BVOW061040130212

282806BV00005B/32/P

9 781449 311568